Where Can I Find God?

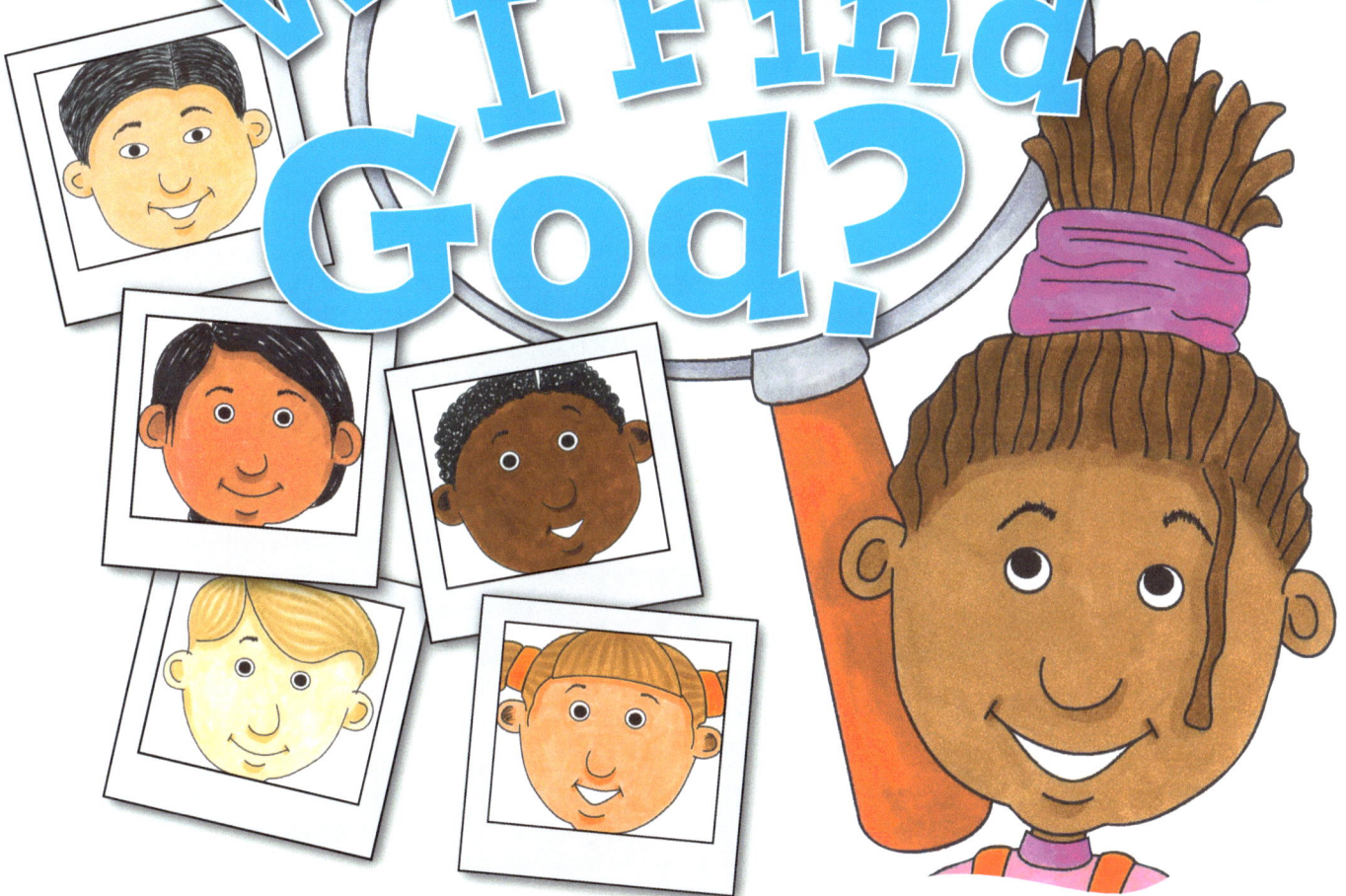

by J. Cecil Anderson

This book features Red Dot•Best Spot™ Page Numbering—a numbering method that utilizes a red dot icon, to serve as a counting aid and guide for young readers when turning book pages. This extends reading enjoyment through proper book care and preservation.

RED DOT•BEST SPOT™
PAGE NUMBERING

I0144070

Written, illustrated and designed by J. Cecil Anderson

Where Can I Find God?
ISBN 978-0-692-80495-7

Scriptures are from the *Holy Bible* (King James Version).

Holy Child
PUBLICATIONS, LLC

P.O. Box 954
Fairburn, Georgia 30213

Manufactured in the U.S.A.

Dedication

To Father God for continually using me in such a wonderful way.
Hallelujah!

To my awesome wife for your endless encouragement which keeps me going.

To the many children with whom I have shared, and will share, the Gospel of Jesus Christ.
Remember…you are more than a conqueror!

To my late grandmother, Naomi Anderson.
Remembering your humbleness and meekness keeps me focused. Thank you.

Acknowledgments

To all who have sown into this great ministry—many thanks and gratitude.
May Father God richly bless and empower you to achieve the desires of your heart.

Today, I am going on a **quest**.
It could be near, or far like a mile.

I am looking to find where God is,
to talk with Him and see His smile.

2

I have heard that God is everywhere, but I have not seen Him at all.

Riiing!

I think I might need a little help. Hey! Someone is giving me a call!

"Hello Sara! Everyone is here…
and wondering what you are doing?"

"Hey Joey! I am glad you called.
I have an adventure that needs **pursuing**."

"Oh! Wow! That sounds great!
We will be there right away.

Naomi, our new neighbor, just stopped by;
now we all will have fun today."

5

"Thanks Joey. See you soon.
I will wait out front by the tree.

6

Be sure to bring your Zip-CAM,
to take pictures of things we see."

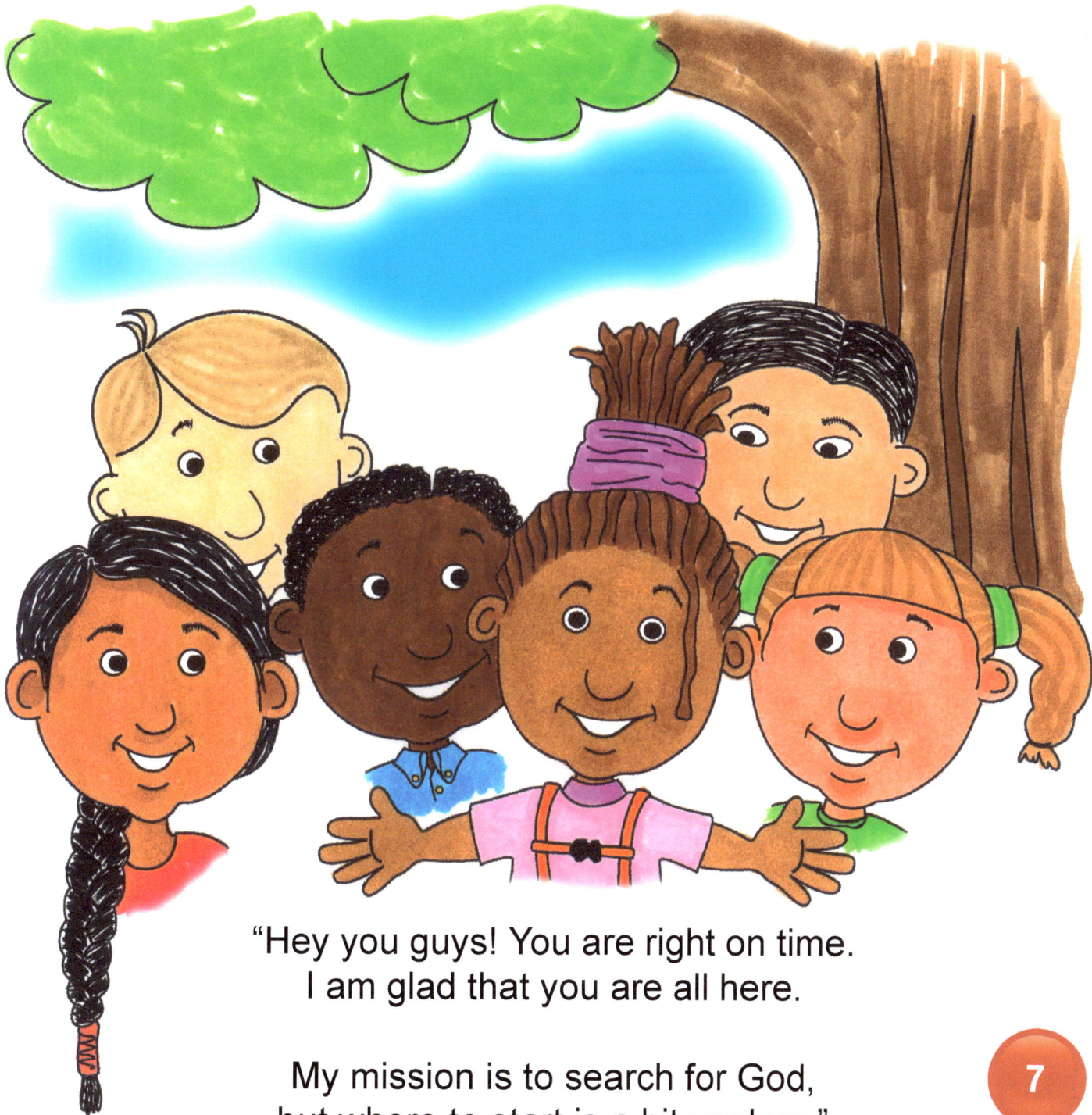

"Hey you guys! You are right on time.
I am glad that you are all here.

My mission is to search for God,
but where to start is a bit unclear."

7

"Let us go see Pastor at the church,"
Maria said as we gathered around.

"I am sure he can help,
he walks with God. He knows where
God can be found."

HOLY PROMISE FAITH CHURCH

Good News...
God Lov   Y

Sunday School
9:30 AM

Worship Service
11:00 AM

Wednesday Service
7:00 PM

"Good Morning Pastor...
I need your help! I want to see God
face-to-face.

I have been told that He is
everywhere, but I have not found a trace."

9

"Yes, yes! I see what you mean," Pastor said then wrote out a list.

"Here are some places that you should check. You will find Him if you **persist**."

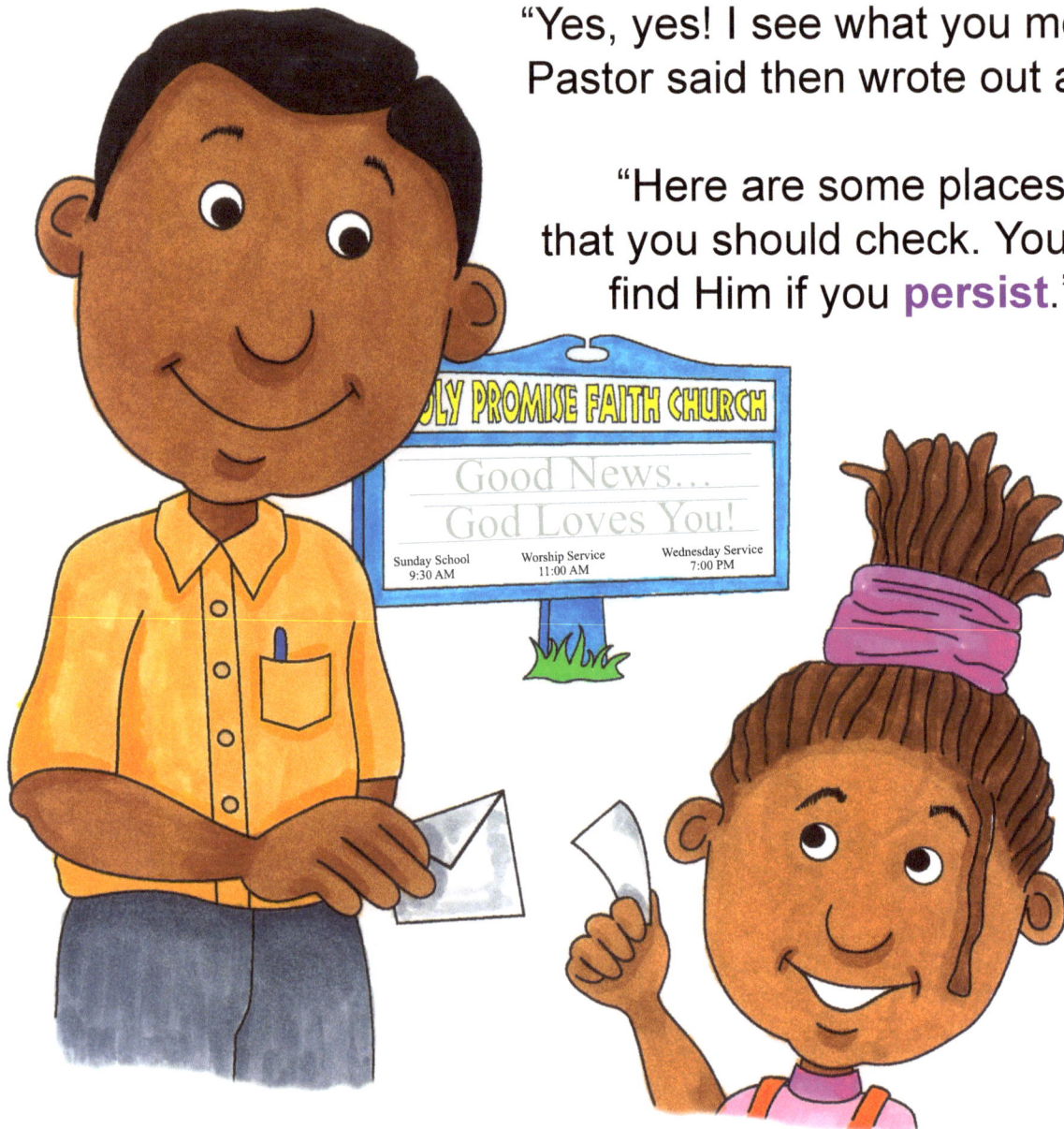

"Before you leave, I ask one favor. It could be a great help to you.

Please take this note to Main Street and deliver it to house 102."

"Okay," we agreed and
thanked our Pastor.
Off we went to where God would be.

First on the list was the grocery store that is **owned** by
Mr. and Mrs. Mawulee.

11

We greeted, then explained our search for God. "Just keep looking!" they both replied.

While there we helped pack boxes of food, for a neighborhood where poor families reside.

The second on the list was our beautiful park,
a place where everyone comes to play.

CITY PARK

Lots of laughing and also sharing…
surely, God visits here every day!

13

Our third stop was Rophe Medical Center…
where everyone shows how much they care.

There are lots of rooms
with lots of beds,
and I think babies come from there.

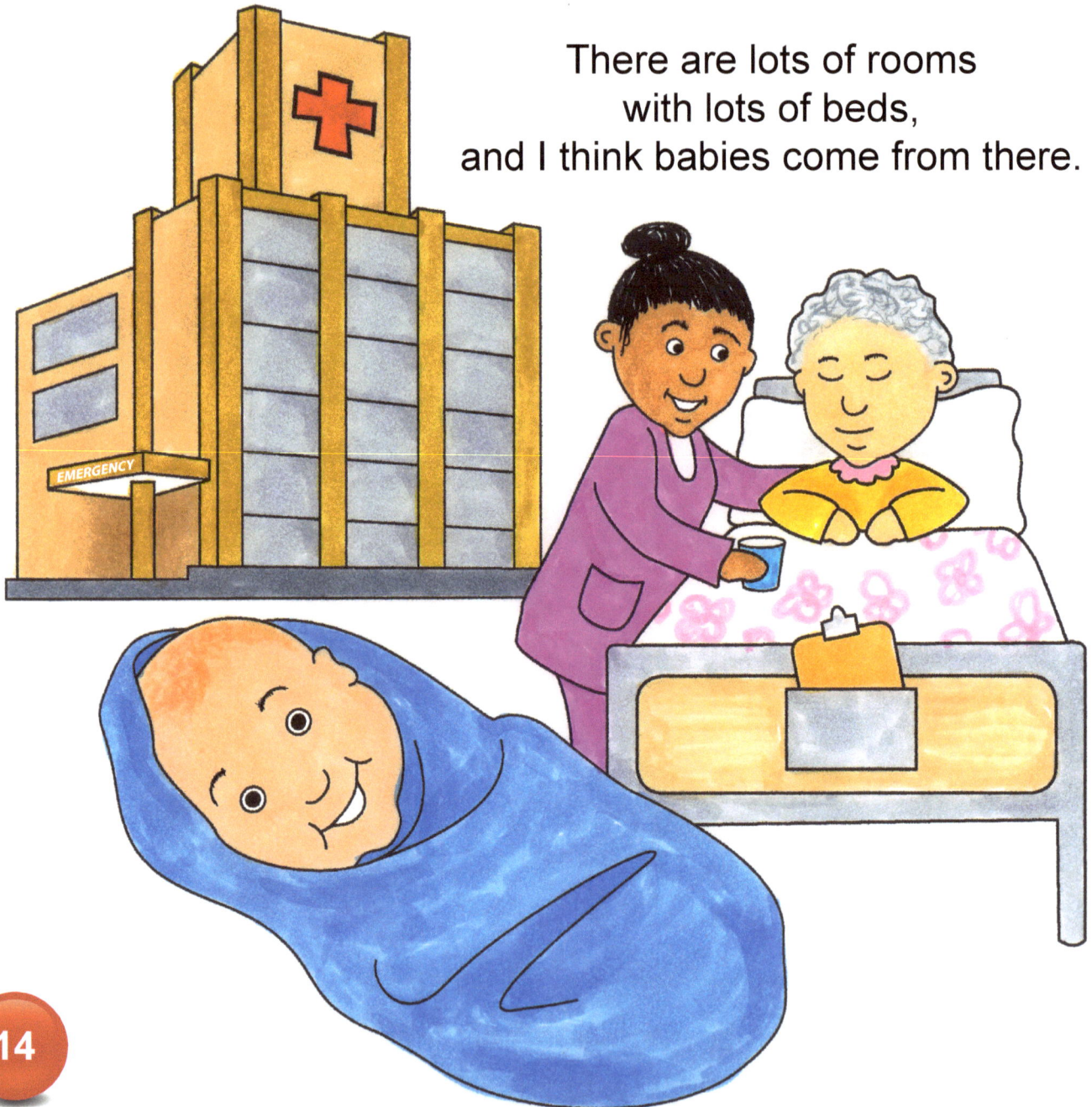

EMERGENCY

The fourth place we went was really cool.
Rosa's Thrift Store is new to our **community**.
We buy things there or **donate** if we choose
and much of the money goes to **charity**.

15

Our fifth stop was the last on the list.
It was the residence of Mr. Jerry.

He is very nice, teaches at our
school and once traveled
as a **missionary**.

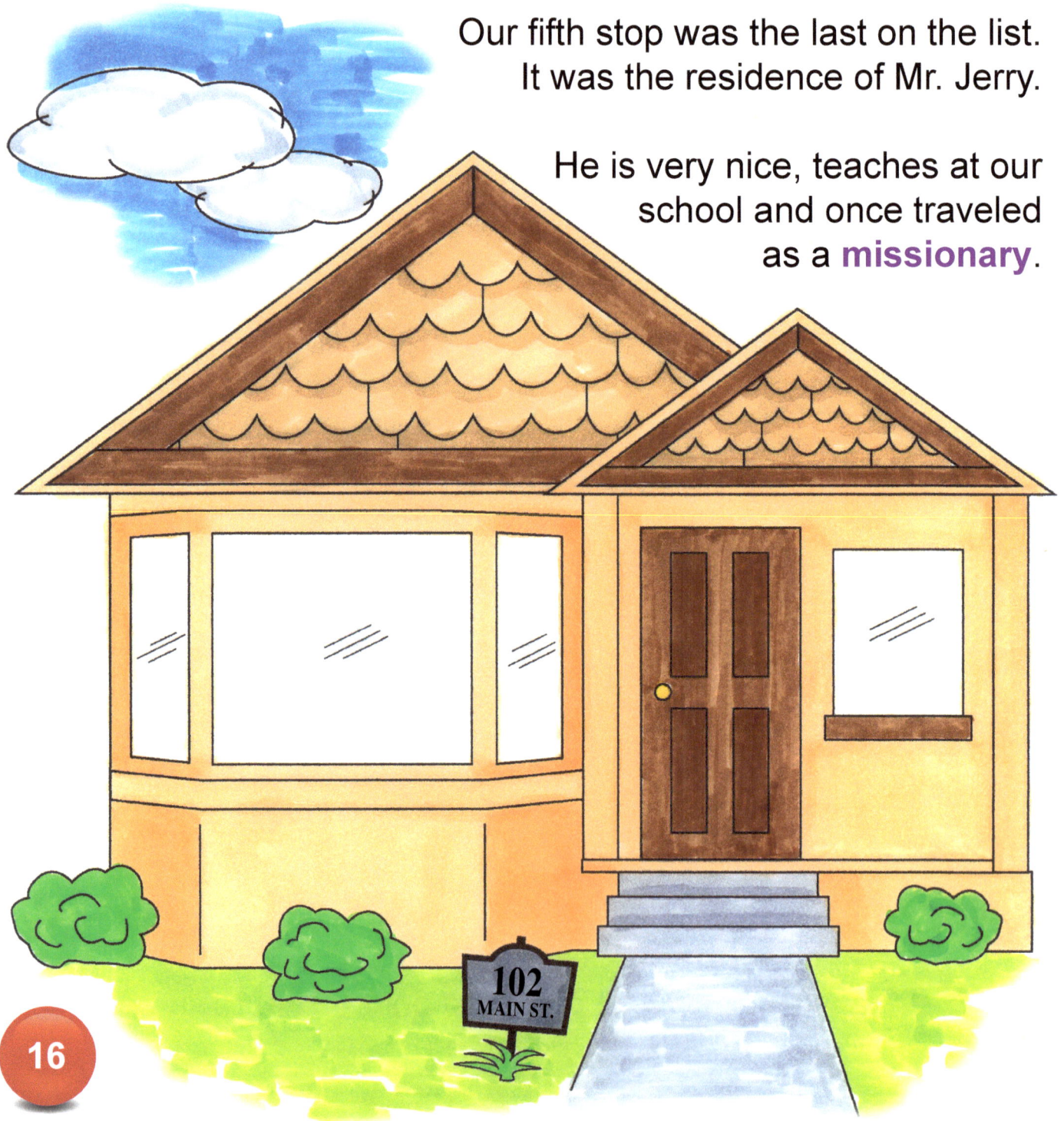

102
MAIN ST.

"Hello my friends, what
brings you here?"
So we gave him the note
Pastor sent.

We explained that we
were looking for God,
and to find Him was our
every **intent**.

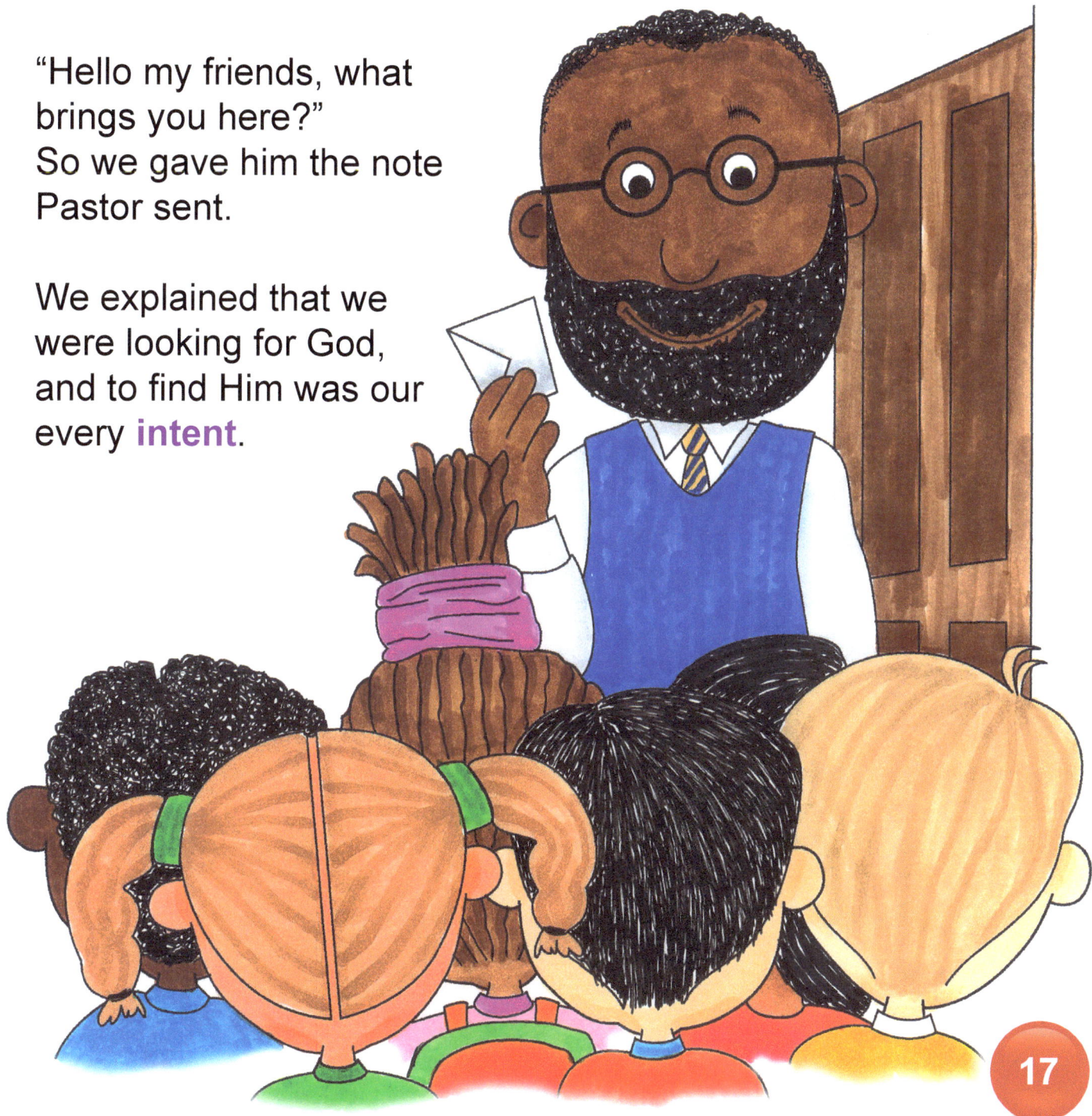

He read the note then smiled and said, "Who you are looking for is in plain sight.
He can be seen through love and caring.
Yes! He is with us each day and every night."

Joy
Compassion
Peace
Kindness

"Whenever we show **concern** for others, Father God is there without a doubt.
Through peace, compassion, kindness and joy, His love surely shines all about."

Okay I get it! God is inside of us,
and He wants us to share love with all.
Now I know where I can find God…
and this I will always recall.

19

Jeremiah 29:13

And ye shall seek me, and find me,
when ye shall search for me with all your heart.

1 John 4:16b

God is love; and he that dwelleth in love dwelleth in God,
and God in him.

See You Later!

21

God's Love Is All Around

There is a word that describes where God is right now. It is omnipresent.
This means God is everywhere at the same time. Though we may not see Him,
His presence is here. Another word that describes God is love. He is love
in the purest form—so where there is Love, there is God.

There are many ways to show and express love, one of which is shown
through charity. Charity occurs when we think kindly about someone in need
then we do something to help them. This is the love of God within us
moving into action. Charity is commonly given when someone does not have
the basic needs for life—such as food, clothing or shelter. Charity also
is given when people experience tragic losses in their lives.

Yes! Charity is happening every moment…of every day…all around the world!
And where there is charity there is GOD.

7 Ways You Can Show Charity

- Start a food drive for needy families at your school or church
  (collect boxed or canned goods)
- Donate good, clean clothes you no longer wear to a thrift store
- Make greeting cards with friends for patients in a nearby hospital
- Visit a senior care home and read to, or sing for, residents there
- Give some of your allowance to help a charitable organization
- Tell someone how much God loves and cares for them
- Pray for the poor and those who are in need

Remember to get permission and help from your parents!

Very, Visible, VOCABULARY

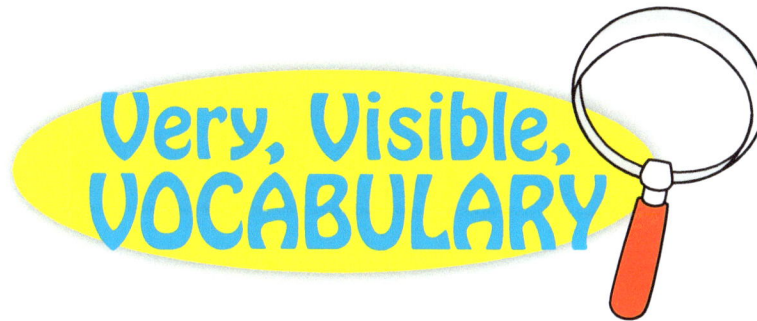

quest: a search or hunt

pursue (pursuing): to follow after in order to reach or catch

persist: to continue in a firm, steady way without stopping or slowing down

own (owned): belonging to; to have possession of by right or law

reside: to live in a place for a long time

community: a particular area where a group of people live

donate: to give something that helps others

charity: kind actions and/or donations for someone in need

missionary: a minister who goes to another country to teach, convert, heal and serve

intent: determined to do something; a focused plan, aim or purpose

concern: a matter that is important to someone

recall: to remember; to bring a past event into the mind

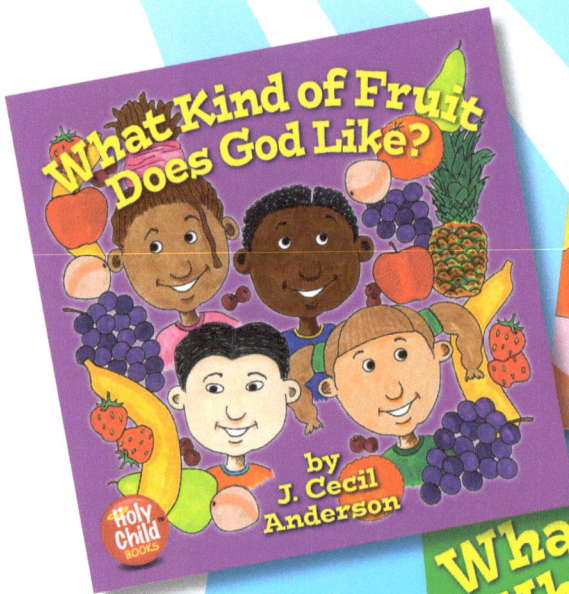

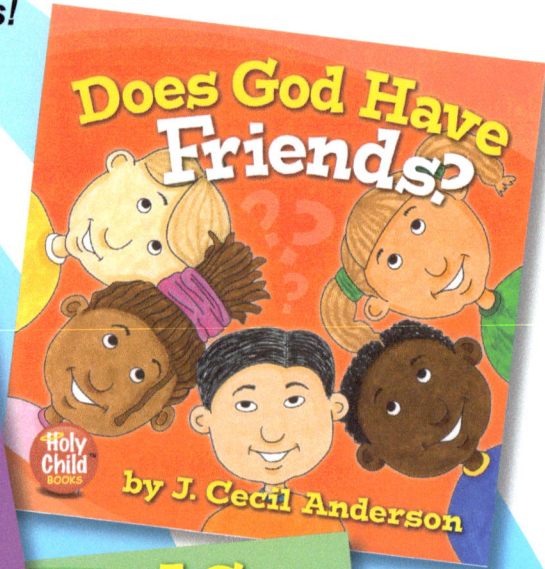

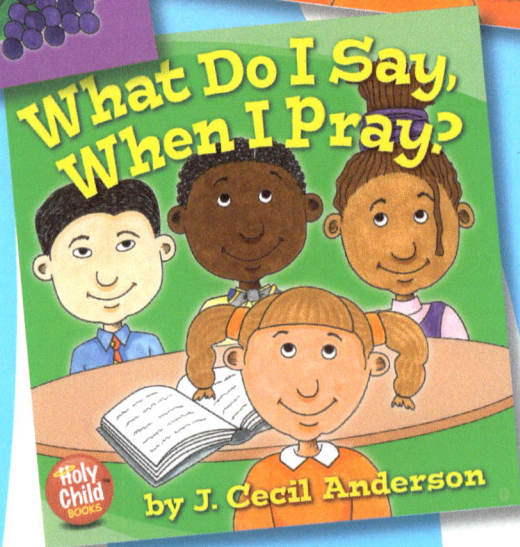

24

www.ingramcontent.com/pod-product-compliance
Lightning Source LLC
Chambersburg PA
CBHW041223040426

42443CB00002B/73